Observation Worksheets

for

Rathus's

Childhood and Adolescence Voyages in Development

Second Edition

Observation Worksheets

for

Rathus's

Childhood and Adolescence Voyages in Development

Second Edition

Debra Schwiesow
Creighton University

THOMSON
WADSWORTH
Australia • Canada • Mexico • Singapore • Spain • United Kingdom • United States

Printed in the United States of America
1 2 3 4 5 6 7 09 08 07 06 05

Printer: Thomson West

ISBN 0-495-03066-X

For more information about our products, contact us at:
Thomson Learning Academic Resource Center
1-800-423-0563

For permission to use material from this text or product, submit a request online at **http://www.thomsonrights.com.**
Any additional questions about permissions can be submitted by email to **thomsonrights@thomson.com.**

Thomson Higher Education
10 Davis Drive
Belmont, CA 94002-3098
USA

Asia (including India)
Thomson Learning
5 Shenton Way
#01-01 UIC Building
Singapore 068808

Australia/New Zealand
Thomson Learning Australia
102 Dodds Street
Southbank, Victoria 3006
Australia

Canada
Thomson Nelson
1120 Birchmount Road
Toronto, Ontario M1K 5G4
Canada

UK/Europe/Middle East/Africa
Thomson Learning
High Holborn House
50–51 Bedford Road
London WC1R 4LR
United Kingdom

Latin America
Thomson Learning
Seneca, 53
Colonia Polanco
11560 Mexico
D.F. Mexico

Spain (including Portugal)
Thomson Paraninfo
Calle Magallanes, 25
28015 Madrid, Spain

Preface

This booklet of activities is intended to accompany *Childhood and Adolescence: Voyages in Development, 2nd edition* by Spencer A. Rathus. For every chapter of the Rathus text you will find one activity to be completed by an individual and one group activity.

Caution:

In a few of activities, you are asked to observe or interview children. It is imperative that you do not conduct such activities unless and until you consult with your instructor about the proper procedures for gaining access to children for such purposes, proper procedures for conducting interviews or observations, and any policies or regulations that your university has regarding such activities. It is important that you follow the proper guidelines.

Table of Contents

Chapter 1
Individual Project
Your Own History

Each of us has a unique beginning and a unique path we follow through development. In this project you will trace your own development from birth to the present including physical, cognitive, and social and emotional development. You may want to interview your parents regarding your prenatal and early development. If possible, interview others in your family such as grandparents, siblings or aunts and uncles. You may also want to look through family photo albums and draw upon your own memories.

Use the following chart to summarize your findings.

	Prenatal	Newborn	Early Childhood	Middle Childhood	Adolescence
Physical					
Cognitive					
Social/Emotional					

Look over your chart and indicate which parts of your development have been fairly stable (e.g., shyness, weight for age) and which have been less stable (e.g., hair color, eyesight, curiosity).

Summarize what you have learned about yourself by completing this project.

Chapter 1
Group Project
The Real World of Children
Naturalistic Group Observation

One of the most famous researchers in children development, Jean Piaget, spent hours and hours observing children in their natural environments. In this project your group will watch children as they really are, in their natural environments. With a group of your classmates observe children in a preschool or daycare setting (be sure you have parental permission for these settings), a mall or a park. As a group decide what you'll be observing. Some ideas might be the number and types of interactions with adults, number and types of interactions with other children, types of play, sharing behavior, aggressive behavior, temper tantrums, etc. Choose only two or three behaviors to observe and make sure you come to an agreement as to what constitutes that behavior (e.g., temper tantrum means whining, crying, lying on ground, or kicking following an adult request or denial of the child's request). Develop a form in which to record your answers. Once you have completed your observations compile your results and answer the following questions:

1. What conclusions can you draw about children using your observational data?

2. How reliable do you think naturalistic observations are?

3. Do you think your presence influenced how these children acted? Give examples.

4. In what ways do you think naturalistic observations can be or should be used to learn more about children?

Chapter 2
Individual Project
Your Family History

Many of our physical and psychological characteristics are inherited. In this project you will trace your family tree back at least to your grandparents (further, if you can) to determine which of these characteristics run in your family. Answer the following questions:

1. What physical characteristics run in your family?

2. Identify any cognitive characteristics that run in your family.

3. What temperament or social characteristics tend to be found in your family?

4. For each of these characteristics you've identified find out if they are primarily determined by heredity, by environment or by a combination of these factors.

5. For those that are primarily determined by heredity find out if these are passed by dominant or recessive genes or by some other genetic process.

6. Does your family have any inherited disorders that run in your family?

7. If there were a genetic test that would provide early detection of these disorders would you want yourself tested? Your spouse? Your unborn child?

8. What would be the pros and cons of knowing that you had an inherited disorder?

Chapter 2
Group Project
The Impact of Infertility

The impact of infertility can be devastating to a couple. In this project you will hear first hand from a couple who is facing infertility. Form several groups within your class and find at least one couple who has faced infertility. Develop a common set of questions to be used by each group using the following as a starting point. After interviewing each of the couples come back together as a class and compare your answers. What are some common themes and what are some unique themes mentioned by these couples? Draw some conclusions about how couples might deal with infertility.

1. When and how did you first learn that you were infertile?

2. What was your initial reaction to this information? Your later reactions?

3. What methods have you used to try and conceive and what have been the results?

4. In what ways do you think infertility has affected your relationship as a couple?

5. How has your family and your friends reacted to your infertility?

6. What advice would you have for couples going through a similar situation?

Chapter 3
Individual Project
Pamphlet for Expectant Mothers: Prenatal Development

First-time expectant mothers are often bombarded with information about what they should do or not do during their pregnancy. In this project you are going to compile a short and concise pamphlet for expectant mothers. In this pamphlet you are to include information regarding prenatal care including nutrition and exercise. You are also to address the issue of common teratogens and the prevention of birth defects. This should only be a two-page pamphlet so you must decide on what would be the most critical information for expectant mothers to have. Include at least five points regarding nutrition and three points regarding exercise. Also include general information regarding teratogens, eight common teratogens and advice regarding how to avoid exposure. Attach your pamphlet below. Be creative!

Chapter 3
Group Project
Health Care Providers for Expectant Mothers:
Critical Advice

What do health care providers consider the most important information for expectant mothers to have? In this project you will find out! Form a group and create a list of health care providers who work with expectant mothers. Some suggestions for providers are OB/GYNs, Nurse Practitioners, Physician Assistants, RNs, Neonatal Intensive Care Nurses, or Midwives. Each group member should contact one of these providers and arrange for a short interview. Come back as a large group to compile and compare your answers. What is similar and what is different?

Below are some questions to get you started but be sure and add your own.

1. Describe your job and what role you play in ensuring the health of expectant mothers and their unborn children?

2. How would you rate the United States in terms of prenatal care? Are there things you would suggest to improve the prenatal care of all expectant mothers?

3. What advice do you give an expectant mother regarding exercise, the use of alcohol, smoking, nutrition and avoiding birth defects?

4. What is the most important advice you could give an expectant mother?

Chapter 4
Individual Project
What Is Childbirth Really Like?

Many expectant mothers prepare for labor and delivery by reading and attending childbirth classes; however, the actual experience of birth may be quite different. Birth preparation and labor and delivery practices have changed somewhat over the years. For this project you will interview your grandmother, mother, aunts, and/or friends regarding their actual birth experiences.

Prenatal Care

1. What type of prenatal care did you receive? When did you start going to see a doctor? What types of prenatal assessments were used?

2. What advice were you given regarding nutrition, exercise, smoking, alcohol, etc.?

3. What other types of advice did your doctors give you?

4. What advice did your friends give you?

Labor and Delivery

1. How did you prepare for labor and delivery?

2. What happened during the actual labor and delivery?

   a. How long did it last?

   b. Was it a vaginal delivery or C-section?

3. What, if any, medications were used?

4. Where your husbands in the room?

5. In what ways did your labor and delivery differ from what you expected?

Postpartum Period

1. How soon after birth were you allowed to see your baby?

2. How long did you stay in the hospital and what advice were you given regarding the postpartum period?

Conclusions

Compare their answers. What differences did you note? What do you think might account for these similarities or differences? What, if any, conclusions can you draw about how prenatal care, labor and delivery and after birth care has changed over the years? This might be an interesting assignment to compare with others in your class.

Chapter 4
Group Project
How Much Does It Cost to Have a Baby?

Babies cost money! But how much? In this project you will find out! Before beginning this assignment have each member of your group estimate how much they think it costs to have a baby (prenatal care, labor and delivery and after birth care). Assign each member to call at least one birth setting (hospital, birthing center, etc.) in your area to gain information regarding current costs for prenatal care, delivery, hospital room, neonatal care, pediatric exam and circumcision. Include the prices for a vaginal delivery and a C-section. Compare and contrast your answers. How does this compare to your estimate?

	Setting 1	Setting 2	Setting 3	Setting 4
Prenatal Care				
Labor and Delivery				
Hospital Room				
Neonatal Care				
Pediatric Exam				
Circumcision				
Other expenses				

As a follow-up to the first part of this project have each member of the group investigate costs that might occur during a baby's first year of life. Such items might include crib and bedding, diapers, clothing from newborn to 12-month size, high chair, stroller, formula, baby food and toys. Include any other items you think might be necessary. Were you surprised? Compare your costs with other groups' costs.

Chapter 5
Individual Project
Breast or Bottle?
Which Would You Choose for Your Baby?

One of the important decisions that new parents need to make is whether to breastfeed or bottle feed their infant. In this project you will gather together information on both methods and come to a conclusion regarding which you would choose. Use the following format to gather your data from journals or reliable internet sources. Put in any additional categories that will help you compare these two feeding methods.

	Breastfeeding	Bottlefeeding
Cost		
Convenience		
Health benefits to mother		
Health benefit to infant		

Summary: Based on the information you've gathered, summarize the pros and cons of breast and bottle feeding. Which would you choose for your baby?

Chapter 5
Group Project
Want or Need?
The Cost of Baby Equipment

Preparing for the care of a newborn baby includes purchasing baby equipment. In this project your group will gather information about the type of equipment babies need (e.g., car seats, high chairs, cribs, baby monitors, etc.) and rate each in terms of their necessity. Is this particular item needed for safety reasons or is it a want on the part of parents (a convenience rather than a necessity)? Use the following chart to record your answers.

Equipment	Need	Want	Cost

Conclusions

Summarize what your group found out about baby equipment. What would be the cost of necessary equipment versus the cost of wanted equipment? What advice would you give new parents regarding this topic?

Chapter 6
Individual Project
What Are They Saying?:
Language Development in Young Children

Infants communicate in various ways. For this project you will record the vocalizations of children in the following age ranges: 0-5 months, 6-10 months and 11-15 months. Interview the parents regarding their child's communications and how they interpret what the child was "saying" during each of your recordings. Summarize your findings in a short paper including the following information:

1. Categorize the vocalizations of children in each of these age groups. How were they the same and how were they different? Identify any characteristics of prelinguistic or linguistic speech you observed.

2. What did the parents say about their child's vocalizations? What did they think their child was trying to communicate? Would you, as an observer, have come to a similar conclusion? Why or why not?

3. If possible, share your recording with the class and see if they can identify the age of the child, communicative intent and characteristics of prelinguistic or linguistic speech.

Chapter 6
Group Project
Object Permanence in Action

The attainment of object permanence is an important step in the cognitive development of infants since it represents an ability to mentally represent an object that previously had to be physically present. In this project you will demonstrate object permanence. Arrange for four different aged infants to come to class to demonstrate the various stages of object permanence acquisition. An alternative would be to videotape this demonstration. If possible, include the following age ranges: 4 to 8 months, 8 to 12 months, 12 to 18 months and 18 to 24 months. Before you begin this project, be sure to consult with your instructor regarding the appropriate ways to observe infants. Use the following task:

1. Show the infant an interesting toy then cover it with a cloth. What does the infant do? Move the cloth to expose a part of the toy. What does the infant do now?

2. Show the infant the toy and move it behind a box or screen. Does the infant search for it?

3. Show the infant the toy, and then cover it with a cloth. Move the toy and the cloth behind a box or screen leaving the toy behind the screen but returning the cloth to the front. What does the infant do? Does the infant look under the cloth or behind the screen?

4. What generalizations can you make about object permanence acquisition based on your observations? Are they similar to Piaget's findings as described in your text? If different, what do you think might account for these differences?

Chapter 7
Individual Project
Differences in Father and Mother Caregiving

Mothers and fathers sometimes differ in the ways they interact with their infants. In this project you will interview a father and mother of an infant regarding the quantity and quality of their caregiving. The goal of this project is to be able to make some general comparisons regarding the similarities and differences of caregiving based on gender.

Some of the questions you could ask include the following (be sure and add your own):

1. What type of caregiving activities do you engage in with your infant (feeding, changing diapers, bathing, holding, rocking, etc.)?

2. What other types of activities do you engage in with you infant?

3. How much time would you estimate you spend with your infant per week in caregiving activities? In other activities?

4. How much time would you estimate your husband/wife spends with your infant per week in caregiving activities? In other activities? How do you think their caregiving differs from yours?

5. Do you see your role as a caregiver to your infant as different from your own mother and father's caregiving. If there are differences what do you think might account for these? Give specific examples.

Summarize your findings below. What conclusions can you draw based on this interview regarding the quantity and quality of time spent in infant care? How does this differ between the mother and the father? What do you think accounts for these differences?

Chapter 7
Group Project
Pink or Blue?

Differences between the sexes are influenced by nature and nurture. Societies and families often dictate what appropriate behavior is for boys and for girls, including play behavior and play objects. The purpose of this project is to determine the similarities and differences between toys for boys and girls in infancy and toddlerhood. Your group should divide up this task and visit a total of 3 toy stores (or you could search for toys on-line). Compare toys for infant and toddlers based on gender specific characteristics. You might want to also briefly look at toys for older age groups. Record such information as color, type of toy, and purpose of toy (e.g., fine motor play, oral stimulation, etc.) Come back together as a group with your information, compile your answers and develop conclusions based on your findings.

	Toy Store #1	Toy Store #2	Toy Store #3
Toys for infant girls			
Toys for infant boys			
Toys for toddler girls			
Toys for toddler boys			

Chapter 7
Group Project (continued)
Pink or Blue?

Conclusions

What overall differences did your group find regarding toys for these age groups based on gender? Were there differences between toys for infants and toys for toddlers based on gender? What factors account for these differences? Were you surprised by any of your findings? In your brief look at toys for older children what did you note in differences between boys' and girls' toys? Write a brief summary below.

Chapter 8
Individual Project
Immunizations Then and Now

Due to advances in medical research and development of new immunizations, the requirements for childhood immunizations have changed over the years. In this project you will compare the types of immunizations your parents received, the types you received and what is required for children today. To find out this information you may want to talk to a pediatric nurse, a pediatrician, explore sites on-line and/or interview others.

	Types of immunizations required
Parents	
You	
Children today	

Summary

1. What types of immunizations are the same across the three groups?

2. What immunizations are different across the three groups?

3. Why do you think immunization requirements have changed over the years?

4. What are some of the pros and cons of these changes?

Chapter 8
Group Project
Gross and Fine Motor Development in Early Childhood

Children in preschool or daycare settings have opportunities to practice both gross and fine motor skills in various ways. In this project your group will observe in a childcare setting and record the types of activities you see that encourage motor development. Along with your observations you should interview the childcare provider regarding other motor activities in which the children engage. Try and observe in at least three settings. Before you begin, be sure to consult with your instructor regarding safely and appropriately observing children, and obtaining the proper permission from preschool administrators.

—	Setting #1	Setting #2	Setting #3
Fine motor activities			
Gross motor activities			

Conclusions:

1. What are some common fine motor activities you observed in these three settings? Do you think these activities are developmentally appropriate for this age group? Why or why not?

2. What are some common gross motor activities you observed in these three settings? Do you think these activities are developmentally appropriate for this age group? Why or why not?

3. Are there any recommendations you would make to these childcare providers regarding other types of activities to encourage healthy motor development in young children?

Chapter 9
Individual Project
Children's Books

Literacy in later years is strongly tied to early exposure to books. For this project you will explore children's books specifically written for children ages two to six. You might want to visit your local library and/or local bookstore and find the section of books for this age group. Find at least eight different books and record your information below. Be sure and add your own questions and/or observations.

1. What are the titles of the books you found?

2. Do you remember any of these books from your childhood?

3. Which of these books do you think are intended for children to read with their parents? Which, if any, do you think are meant to be read independently?

4. Which of these books would you want your own children to read? Why?

5. What are the general themes of these books?

6. How many of these books involve animals as the main characters? Humans?

7. In what ways do you think the book's illustrations are used to engage a young reader? What other methods are used?

8. How do you think these books encourage overall cognitive development in young children?

9. What conclusions can you draw regarding the use of books to encourage literacy and cognitive development in young children?

Chapter 9
Group Project
Take a Side: Could We or Should We Create Superbabies?

One of the controversial topics regarding child rearing is how much and in what ways parents should be involved in encouraging children's cognitive development. For this project your group will take both sides of this issue and debate this in class.

Pro: It is important for parents to educate their children as early as possible and as much as possible. Young children are capable of absorbing more than we think and therefore it is up to the parents to provide early education for their children.

Con: Young children naturally create their own learning opportunities and learn at a fairly predictable timetable based on maturation. Too much push towards education unduly creates anxiety and competition.

Research each of these topics and create a list of arguments supporting each side.

Chapter 10
Individual Project
Family Birth Order

There is some evidence (although not conclusive) that your birth order within your family may affect your personality. In this project you will gather some of your own information and come to conclusions based on your data. Before beginning your project find information in your text and other resources regarding what the research says about the characteristics of first-born children, middle-born children, last-born children, and only children. Then gather data about members of your family: you, your siblings, your parents, their siblings, cousins, etc. Does your data match what the research says about birth order?

1. Research information regarding characteristics of first-born children.

2. Research information regarding characteristics of last-born children.

3. Research information regarding characteristics of middle-born children.

4. Research information regarding characteristics of only children.

5. Other relevant information.

Person	Birth Order	Characteristics that fit with the research	Characteristics that don't fit with the research

Conclusions: In what ways does your data match research data? In what ways does it not? Can you make any clear conclusions relating birth order with personality?

Chapter 10
Group Project
TV Watching and Young Children

TV watching has been linked with increased violence in children, obesity and poor reading ability. On the other hand some TV programs provide positive role models and academic stimulation. In this project your group will watch TV shows geared towards young children (ages 2 to 6) and come to your own conclusions. Is TV watching a positive or negative influence on young children?

As a group choose at least three programs from each of these categories: educational programming, prime-time shows and cartoons. If possible, watch the entire program and rate them in the following categories but be sure and add any other categories you think are relevant.

Name of show	Type of show (prime-time, educational or cartoon)	General theme or message of show	Number and types of aggressive acts towards others and toward objects	Number and types of prosocial acts	Content of commercials	Gender stereotypes	Opportunity for interaction

Chapter 10
Group Project (continued)
TV Watching and Young Children

Conclusions

1. Which of these shows do you think would be appropriate for young children? Support your answer with examples.

2. Based on your sample draw some conclusions regarding the possible link between TV watching and aggression and TV watching and obesity. Give examples.

3. What recommendations would you give to parents regarding the shows included in your study? TV watching in general?

4. What recommendations would you give to the media regarding programming for young children?

Chapter 11
Individual Project
Health in Middle Childhood

One of the growing concerns regarding children is obesity caused by limited exercise and poor nutrition. In this project you will gather together data regarding recommended diet and activity level for children in this age group (6 – 12 year olds) and then interview a child and/or parent regarding actual diet and activity level. Compare these sources, what did you find? Before you begin, be sure to consult with your instructor regarding the proper procedures for conducting an interview with a child.

First you will need to find what is recommended for middle-aged children in terms of caloric intake and types and quantity of food needed to support good health. You may want to contact a pediatrician's office, a clinical nutritionist at a local hospital and/or search the internet for reliable information. Also, find out from these sources what would be recommended for amount and type of activity needed for this age group.

When interviewing a parent and/or child be sensitive to the fact that an interview format can lead to faulty information (subjects sometimes answer the way in which they think is socially acceptable such as overestimating the amount of activity in which a child engages).

Write your conclusions and summary below: How do these two/three sources compare? In what ways are they the same and in which ways are they different? What recommendations, if any, would you give to the parents of this child regarding nutrition and exercise?

Chapter 11
Individual Project (continued)
Health in Middle Childhood

	Medical Source (pediatrician, nurse, nutritionist, internet)	Parent	Child
Average calories that should be or are consumed in a day			
Types of food that should be or are consumed in a day (list type and amount) [You might want to ask what the child had to eat that day and the day before.]			
Average amount of time (in minutes per day) that should be or are spent in active play			
Types of activity that should be or are engaged in on a weekly basis [What types and how often.]			
Approximate weight (ideal versus actual)			

Chapter 11
Group Project
Organized Sports: Take a Side

Little League sports are popular in the United States. But are they good for children or should children be allowed to be involved in spontaneous and non-competitive sports? Take a side and debate it in class.

Pro: Organized sports such as Little League are good for children in middle childhood.

Con: Children in middle childhood are better off organizing their own games and participating in more non-competitive sports.

Here are some thoughts to get your groups started but be sure and add your own opinions.

Pro:

1. The large number of children involved in Little League sports reflects its success. Children would not participate in these types of sports if they did not want to.
2. Little League provides an outlet for children and keeps them "off the streets" and out of trouble after school.
3. Little League helps connect parents and children in a common activity.
4. Competition is a way of life in the USA therefore Little League helps prepare children for competition in later life.
5. Organized sports help curb obesity.

Con:

1. Children begin competitive sports too early, when they are not physically or cognitively adept at performing these types of sports.
2. Children at this age have difficulty understanding the often complex rules of competitive sports.
3. Physical activity in organized sports in a lot less than physical activity exerted during spontaneous games.
4. In spontaneous sports children must learn to develop rules, compromise and settle conflicts on their own; in Little League the rules are generally inflexible and conflicts are handled by adults.
5. Parents can become too over-critical of their child's performance during Little League sports therefore demeaning a child's self-esteem and self-confidence.

Chapter 12
Individual Project
Intelligence in Children: Is It Only a Score?

Many misnomers exit regarding intelligence. In this project you will find out more about intelligence tests and what they actually show about a child's intelligence and ability to be successful in school.

All school districts are required to either hire or have access to a school psychologist. School psychologists are mental health professionals whose primary role is to ensure that all children receive an adequate education regardless of ability or disability. As a part of their graduate program school psychologists are trained to give individual IQ tests to help in understanding a child's strengths and weaknesses in learning and to help identify what educational strategies might be effective. Contact your local school psychologist and interview them about the use and misuse of IQ tests. You could also contact a local university that offers a graduate program in school psychology and interview one of the professors in that department.

Summarize your findings in a two to three-page paper.

Here are some questions to get you started:

1. In what situations would you give a child an individual IQ test?

2. What are IQ tests meant to show about a child's intelligence?

3. What are some of the myths about IQ tests and how can IQ tests be misused?

4. What are some alternative concepts of intelligence?

5. How are IQ and academic success in school related?

6. What recommendations would you give to parents who have been asked for their permission to give their child an IQ test? What would they need to know before they give their permission?

Chapter 12
Group Project
Concrete Operations in Action

Erik Erikson proposed that children in middle childhood were in the concrete operations stage of cognitive development. Concrete operations involves conservation, transitivity, and class inclusion. In this project your group members will have a child in concrete operations stage (generally 6-11) and a child in pre-operational stage (generally 3-5) demonstrate their understanding of each of these concepts.

Your group should design a consistent task that could demonstrate a child's understanding of conservation, transitivity and class inclusion. Use your text as a starting place for ideas along with information obtained from the internet for examples of tasks. You may choose to bring these children into class or videotape their responses. Be able to explain what you see and hear in terms of how Erikson would describe their cognitive processes. What in these children's responses clearly demonstrates concrete operational thought processes and what demonstrates pre-operational thought proccsses? Use the table below to record the task you'll be using and the child's response. Before you begin, be sure to consult with your instructor regarding the appropriate way to observe children in this way and obtaining permission to do so.

Type of task (describe task presented)	Concrete operational child (if and how child demonstrated understanding of this concept)	Preoperational Child (if and how child demonstrated understanding of this concept)
Conservation		
Transitivity		
Class inclusion		

Chapter 13
Individual Project
Children in Stepfamilies: How Do They Fare?

Data show that most divorced people remarry which means that many children in the United States will become a part of a stepfamily. For this project you will gather data from stepfamilies you know and come to your own conclusions based on your sample. How do children fare in stepfamilies?

To gather this data you will interview the parents and children (if possible) and use the following questions as a part of your interview. Be sure and add your own questions. Before you begin, be sure to consult with your instructor regarding the appropriate ways to interview children and obtaining permission to do so.

Parents' Questions

1. How old were your children when you divorced? Remarried?

2. How do you think your divorce affected your children? In what ways do you think your remarriage has affected your children?

3. How have your children adapted to having a stepparents, stepsiblings or half-siblings?

4. What role does your current spouse play in your children's lives? What role does the other biological parent play in your children's lives?

5. Overall, how well do you think your family is functioning?

6. What advice would you give to other stepfamilies?

Chapter 13
Individual Project (continued)
Children in Stepfamilies: How Do They Fare?

Child Interview

1. How old were you when your parents divorced? Remarried?

2. Do you know anyone else whose parents are divorced? Remarried?

3. What are some of the good things about being a part of a stepfamily? What are some of the not so good things?

4. How do you get along with your stepfather/stepmother and stepsiblings or half-siblings? What things do you like to do with each of them?

5. What advice would you give another child who is about to become a part of a stepfamily?

Conclusions: Based on the information you gathered come to a conclusion regarding the affect stepfamilies may have on children. How is this child faring in their stepfamily?

Chapter 13
Group Project
Popular, Unpopular and Neglected Children: What Can Be Done?

Friendships in middle childhood provide needed socialization, a way to gain self-esteem, and a social and emotional outlet outside of the family. Social status is determined by many factors and may have implications for later development. In this project your group will survey an elementary classroom (2nd – 5th). Be sure to consult with your instructor, and obtain parent and school permission before beginning. Be sure and keep all of the responses confidential.

Ask each child in the class to write down the names of three children in their class whom they would invite to a party and three they would not. Tally the names of the children in the class that made the "invite" list most often (these are likely the popular children), those listed most often as "do not invite" (these are likely the unpopular children), and those not listed (these are likely the neglected children).

Develop a list of characteristics and have the teacher check off characteristics of each of the children who made one of the three lists. Some of the characteristics might include: affectionate, considerate, generous, healthy, original thinkers, self-confident, dependable, and physically attractive, withdrawn, rebellious, aggressive, hostile, immature, lacking in confidence, unattractive and slow learners.

How do these characteristics relate to what you read in the text about popular or unpopular children? What do you think parents and teachers do to help children who are unpopular or neglected? Write a summary of your findings below.

Chapter 14
Individual Project
Eating Disorders: Up Close and Personal

Many adolescents, primarily girls, are at risk for developing an eating disorder sometime during the adolescent period. What are some of the factors that might lead up to the development of an eating disorder and what can be done to treat these disorders? In this project you will interview someone who has or has had an eating disorder. Based on this interview develop a profile of that individual and give some recommendations regarding prevention. Below are some questions to get you started but be sure and add your own.

1. Tell me a little about yourself. What are some things you like to do? What do you think are your strengths and weaknesses as a person?

2. What type of eating disorder do you or did you have?

3. When and how did you first realize that you had an eating disorder? When did your family first realize? When do you think you actually started to develop an eating disorder?

4. What are some of the symptoms you experienced with your eating disorder?

5. What type of treatment are you or did you receive? How successful has it been?

6. What do you think are going to be the short-term and long-term effects of having an eating disorder on your physical and psychological health?

7. What do you think could have prevented you from developing an eating disorder?

8. What advice would you give someone who is experiencing an eating disorder? What advice would you give their family?

Chapter 14
Individual Project (continued)
Eating Disorders: Up Close and Personal

Summarize: Based on your interview develop a brief profile of this individual; who are they as a person? What are some of the symptoms and treatment of their eating disorder? Are these typical? In your opinion what caused this person to develop an eating disorder and what could have been done to prevent it?

Chapter 14
Group Project
Substance Abuse: How Prevalent Is It?

The perception of many is that substance abuse, specifically alcohol abuse, is rampant on college campuses. In this project you will conduct a survey of college students, compile your findings and come to a conclusion regarding the prevalence of alcohol use and abuse. You will then compare it to figures found in research articles and/or web sites.

As a group develop a short, informal questionnaire about alcohol use. Each group member should interview at least 10 people on campus and bring back their data to the group. Your questions might include the following:

1. During a typical week how many alcoholic drinks, if any, do you consume? How many drinks do you think the average student on this campus has during a week?

2. At what age did you start drinking?

3. With whom do you usually drink?

4. Do you tend to have many drinks at one sitting or have drinks more spread out during the evening?

5. How much of a problem do you think alcohol use is on this campus?

6. What do you think could be or should be done to address alcohol use or abuse on our campus?

Chapter 14
Group Project (continued)
Substance Abuse: How Prevalent Is It?

Conclusions: Tally your answers and come up with some data. How many drinks does the "average" student consume during a typical week? What is the average age when drinking begins? Etc. What are your conclusions? How big of a problem do you think alcohol use and abuse is on your campus? What do you think should be done to address alcohol use on your campus? Write a brief summary below.

Chapter 15
Individual Project
Who Was Your Imaginary Audience?

One of the hallmarks of adolescent thinking related to egocentrism is referred to as the imaginary audience, the belief that others are intensely concerned with an adolescent's appearance and behavior and are scrutinizing their every move. Research shows that this belief generally peaks during eighth grade and declines during the rest of adolescence.

What do you remember about this period of your life? Identify specific situations in which you felt that others were scrutinizing you. Do you remember how you felt about this? In what ways did this change your behavior? How and why do you think this belief changed? Write a brief reflection paper below. How do your experiences compare with those discussed in your textbook?

Chapter 15
Group Project
What Risks Are You Willing to Take?

One of the characteristics of adolescent thinking is referred to as the personal fable ("It won't happen to me."). The personal fable is related to risk-taking behaviors such as driving too fast, engaging in unprotected sex, smoking, drinking, etc. In this project you will survey high school students to determine what, if any, types of risk-taking behaviors in which they engage. Be sure to consult with your instructor, and obtain parent and school permission before beginning. Be sure and keep all of the responses confidential. As a group compile your answers and summarize your findings. What risks are adolescents willing to take? Here are some sample questions you might use:

1. What are some things you and friends like to do together?

2. What things do you think teenagers could do that would be considered risky? List as many as you can think of. [If the interviewee has difficulty coming up with examples, you might want to give some suggestions.]

3. Which, if any, of these behaviors have you engaged in within the last month? Last year?

4. Do your friends or anyone you know engage in any of these behaviors? Which ones?

5. What do you think might some of the consequences of some of these behaviors?

6. What's the likelihood that some of these consequences might affect you? Your friends?

Chapter 15
Group Project (continued)
What Risks Are You Willing to Take?

Summary: As a group write a short paper summarizing your findings. What conclusions can you draw from your sample of adolescents? Did you see evidence of risk-taking and/or the personal fable?

Chapter 16
Individual Project
Who Were Your Friends?

Friendships in adolescence provide an important function in terms of social and identity development. Friends can also contribute to a positive self-concept. In this project you will take a look at your friends during high school and your friends now and determine what role they have played in who you are today. Consider the following questions:

1. List your three closest friends during high school.

2. For each of these friends list the characteristics that were most like you and the characteristics that were least like you. Why do you think you were or are friends?

3. For each of these friends identify what types of activities you did together.

4. Which of these friends from high school do you still consider friends? If they are no longer friends, why not?

5. List your three closest friends during college.

6. For each of these friends list the characteristics that are most like you and least like you. Why do you think you are or were friends?

7. For each of these friends identify what types of activities you do or did together.

8. How did your friendships in high school differ from those you have (or had) in college?

9. What role do you think friendships have had in shaping who you are today?

Chapter 16
Group Project
Sex Education in the Schools: Pros and Cons

Sex education in the schools is a controversial issue. Current law requires any discussion about sex focus on abstinence-only or schools could face a loss of funds. What do you think? How should sex education be handled by the schools? Should sex education be entirely a family issue? Divide into two groups and take one side, pro or con. Develop your points by researching your side and lead a debate in class.

Pro: Sex education is best taught in the schools by trained professionals who can provide factual as well as developmentally appropriate information.

Con: Sex education is best handled within the family who can provide factual as well as moral information that fits with the family's beliefs.